Analyzing Notes in the Book of John: John's Contribution to the New Testament Scriptures

Notes in the New Testament, Volume 4

Bible Sermons

Published by Seminit Publications, 2023.

While every precaution has been taken in the preparation of this book, the publisher assumes no responsibility for errors or omissions, or for damages resulting from the use of the information contained herein.

ANALYZING NOTES IN THE BOOK OF JOHN: JOHN'S CONTRIBUTION TO THE NEW TESTAMENT SCRIPTURES

First edition. March 4, 2023.

Copyright © 2023 Bible Sermons.

Written by Bible Sermons.

Table of Contents

"Yo me he hecho solamente esta pregunta: ¿He Nacido De Nuevo ? e instó a que cada uno de ustedes a que se examine honestamente sobre este asunto de extrema importancia. No hemos de quedarnos satisfechos a menos de que en verdad sepamos que así es. ¡Que cosa tan terrible sería que dudara si soy un hijo de Dios o no, si estoy en el camino del cielo o no! ¡Que Dios nos conceda que ninguno de nosotros tenga tal duda, ni siquiera por una hora, sino que tengamos absoluta certeza sobre este punto, por misterioso que sea!".

— **Charles Spurgeon**

Introduction

The apostle John is second only to Paul in his contribution to the New Testament scriptures. For several reasons we accept that he is the author of the fourth Gospel, not the least of which is his intimate knowledge of the Lord himself, 2.24, 4.1, 19.28, and of the holy land, 1.28, 2.1, 3.23. Moreover, he knows the disciples in a special way, giving evidence that he was an eyewitness, 1.40, 6.8.

But John makes no mention of himself. When we consider the specific way in which he names the persons, we have to conclude that it is he who is not named in 13:23 ("one of the disciples, whom Jesus loved"), 20:2 ("the other disciple" ran to the tomb), etc. If someone else had written this Gospel, it would have been strange to omit the name of a person as well known as the apostle John.

The Gospel was written towards the end of the 1st century when John was of advanced age. He remembers in detail the glorious days of his youth when he walked with the Son of God. His is the last of the Gospels and he takes it for granted that his readers are already aware of certain notorious facts. He defines the motive of his narrative: as "that believing, you may have life in his name", 20.30, 31.

From the abundance of material available, the apostle carefully chooses certain details, so that we believe that Jesus is the fulfillment of the ancient prophecies, and more than this, the Son of God. For John, the Messiah has the nature of God himself and by believing in him men can rejoice in the possession of eternal life.

The passage 21.24, 25 can be seen as a brief summary of the Gospel: "This is the disciple who testifies to these things, and he wrote these things; and we know that his testimony is true. And there are also many other things which Jesus did, which if they were written one by one, I think that even the world would not contain the books to be written. Amen. He reminds us of John's reliable testimony and of the wonder of Christ, for in recording all that he did, the world could not contain it. If 20:30, 31 says that he wrote that we might believe for a blessing, these two verses say that he wrote his testimony and the fullness of his inexhaustible theme.

John employs a restricted vocabulary, using the same words over and over again. Nevertheless, he has a profound discernment of the peculiarity of divine revelation in Christ.

We can know it as the structure of the Gospel:

- The Person stated in chapters 1 to 4

- Its power contested in 5 to 12

- His passion described in 13 to 21.

Chapter 1.1 to 14
The Word

———

We know that John was a fisherman, and at the beginning of his Gospel he takes us into deep waters. He refers to our Lord as the Word, the Word, and in so doing says something of his pre-existence. The Word dwelt with God, a fact which makes known his very personality and also the delight the Father had in him. As the Word, he can give expression to God, since he partakes of the essence of his nature.

Having written of his superiority over creation, John says that the Lord came into his own world but his own people did not welcome him. Having entered the world, he was rejected by the Jews but received by certain individuals. By simply accepting him, they became children of God. This theme of revelation, rejection and reception is one that recurs in this Gospel.

John refers to believers as sons of God, emphasizing the new relationship. For John there is only One who is the Son of God, 1.18. However, the Godhead has collaborated to make us sons:

- From God the Father, *1 John 3.1*: *See what love the Father has given us,*

so that we may be called children of God.

- Of the Son, John 1.12: *... gave them authority to become children of God.*

- Of the Spirit, **Romans 8.16**: *The Spirit itself bears witness to our spirit,* *that we are children of God.*

By accepting Christ, we have been born into the family of God by a divine act, 1.13. This birth has nothing to do with blood (descent), nor flesh (desire), nor male (design), but with God (deity), so that believers become partakers of the divine nature, **2 Peter 1.4.**

The Word, not ceasing to be what he always was, became what he had never been, flesh, and tabernacled among us, 1.14. His glory was displayed, and John goes on to speak of this unique glory of the only begotten Son of God. Throughout his Gospel, he sees in Christ the fulfillment of the Old Testament tabernacle:

Door at 14.6,

The copper altar at 1.29,

The source in chapter 3,

The table in chapter 6,

The lamp in chapter 9,

The altar for incense in chapters 14 to 17

The ark of the covenant in 1.1.

Only John speaks of Christ as the only begotten. It is an expression that carries the idea of uniqueness and deep affection, as we perceive in the Old Testament: "Take now your son, your only son, Isaac, whom you love; you did not refuse me your son, your only son," **Genesis 22.2, 12**, *"from my mother's womb, you are my God,"* **Psalm 22.10**; *"mourn as for an only son,"* **Jeremiah 6.26**. The Lord Jesus is full of grace and truth, a further affirmation of His deity: **Exodus 34.6**, "Jehovah.... great in mercy and truth".

Chapter 1.15 to 51
Found to Find

John the Baptist is faithful in his testimony to Christ, and it is not long before others accept the Savior. The section is rich in its many descriptions of the Lord Jesus Christ; 1.17, the One through whom came grace and truth. The law was given by Moses and brought with it the knowledge of sin. It says "do," but grace says, "believe." He is the only begotten Son, who fully expresses the Father and was known as Jesus, 1.18, 29, 36, etc.

He is Lord, but the Baptist points to Him as the Lamb of God, 1.23, 29, 36, a hint that His work is efficacious in its attention to sin. At his baptism he is pointed out as the Son of God, a truth imparted to Nathaniel also, when the latter recognized the superior knowledge of Christ, 1.34, 49. He is the Christ, the true Messiah, and the Son of Man, 1.41, 51, as well as King of Israel, another title emphasizing his Deity; see 1.49 and *Zephaniah 3.15, "Jehovah is King of Israel in the midst of you."* Twice in the section he is referred to as the Rabbi, or Teacher; may we be willing to receive his instruction!

The characters presented are very interesting. John the Baptist takes the attention away from himself and directs it to Christ. John was a voice; Christ is the Word, 1.23, 1. Andrew is challenged, "What do you seek?" This question makes us consider our own motive for following the Lord. Do we follow Him? The supreme question is why. Simon is led to Jesus by his brother Andrew. Peter turns out to be the captain of the boat, 21.3, and Andrew the rafter, always bringing some to Christ, 6.9, 12.20 to 22. John himself stresses the importance of not only coming to Christ but dwelling with him. Philip is located and called by the Lord, and in turn finds his friend Nathanael, who is amazed at the absolute wisdom of the Son of God.

We must reflect on whether we are willing to be just a link in the chain that leads souls to Christ. There is a beautiful sequence here in terms of personal testimony. First the Baptist cries out, "Behold the Lamb of God"; then Andrew and Philip affirm, "We have found"; and finally Philip invites, "Come and see". All three elements are present: declaration, testimony and invitation. There is no better approach.

Chapter 2.1 to 11
The First Signal

It was an occasion of rejoicing that Christ chose as the background for His first miracle. John clearly remembers the outstanding day when a certain wedding took place in Cana of Galilee. The Lord was a man of sorrows but He also knew how to rejoice with those who rejoiced. The next sign in chapter 4, when the centurion's son was healed, is associated with sorrow. Whether seasons of rejoicing or sorrow, it is Lord. How interesting it is to note that he did not perform his first miracle in the capital but in a remote village. It is so characteristic of him to order events in this way and in this we see his great humility and entire lack of ostentation.

The Lord proved to be an ideal host, and the best way to begin married life is to be in His presence! Since all the wine had been distributed, He proved to be more than able to meet the need. John explains very simply that he changed the water into wine, thus symbolizing the displacement of the former washing of Judaism by the superior, inner joy that only Christ can give; *"in thy presence is fullness of joy; delights at thy right hand for evermore"*, **Psalm 16.11**; *"we glory in God through our Lord Jesus Christ"*, **Romans 5.11.** We observe that the wine followed the water; from it proceeded and surpassed it!

John speaks of the Lord's miracles as signs, that is, miracles with a message. In this first sign he dispenses with the long process involved in the production of wine, and by his word alone the Lord directly changes the water into wine, and of the best quality. The consequence of this manifestation was a deeper faith on the part of the disciples.

Others saw this great event happen but in reality it was only the disciples who received the benefit. Others may be affected by it, but only those who love and trust him really learn the truth about his person.

It is instructive to note who was present. We note John's respect for the mother of Jesus: 2.1, 3,5, 19.25, 27. She had implicit confidence in his ability and word. The servants obeyed Christ's words literally and promptly, without question. Do these details characterize our service? The steward was unaware of the miracle but his subordinates knew of the great transformation. Knowledge of Christ is the starting point of true wisdom, *Colossians 2:3.* Finally, with this manifestation of His glory the disciples had a wider appreciation of Him whom they had followed. How much do I esteem His glory and grace?

Chapter 2.12 to 25
Severity and Sincerity of Christ

———

At the Passover the Lord publicly condemns those who make business of religion. According to the prophecy of *Malachi 3:1*, he comes suddenly to his temple in judgment. Some are interested in Christianity only for what they can get out of it. Beware; let us remember Judas. We note that the Lord made a scourge of cords. It was necessary to cleanse the temple but the scourging was not a permanent feature of his ministry. It was not the only occasion when he purged the temple, but we note here his kindness as well as his severity.

The disciples realized their zeal for God's house; compare 2:17 *with Psalm 69:9*: *"I was consumed with zeal for your house; and the reproaches of those who reviled you fell upon me."*

We do well to ask ourselves if we share some of the Lord's zeal for his house, something that directly affects our contribution to the constitution and conduct of the local church,

1 Timothy 3.15. We have to distinguish between an enthusiast and a fanatic. The fanatic has a hot head and a warm heart, but the enthusiast has a balanced head and a burning heart!

Other references to divine zeal are, "Phinehas...shall have the covenant of the priesthood perpetually, because he was zealous for his God," *Numbers 25.13*; *"there shall come out of Jerusalem a remnant...the zeal of the LORD of hosts shall do this,"* **2 Kings 19.31**; *"the increase of his government and peace shall have no end...the zeal of the LORD of hosts shall do this,"* **Isaiah 9.7**.

If the Father was not at home in the temple building, he did find a place in Christ, 2.19. The Lord speaks of his resurrection, and only after this did his disciples understand the meaning of his words, 2.22. When he said, "I will destroy the temple, and in three days I will raise it up," 2.19, the Jews misunderstood him. Later, his opponents misquoted him, *Matt. 26.61, 27.40*. He often spoke on a higher plane than what men generally grasp. He meant something radically different about the birth in chapter 3, the water in chapter 4, the bread in chapter 6, and the temple in this chapter.

Are we grasping what he is saying, or are we thinking and acting merely like carnal men?

Even though Jesus did not respond to the challenges of the Jews to perform an authentic miracle, He did perform many that are not reported by John. Even though many believed in Him, He did not trust them. Why? Because he knew them. Their interest was in what He did and not in Him, 2.23. It was the faith of the curious and not of the committed. He had no faith in their faith. His attitude toward us is based on His infallible knowledge, 2.24, 25; He has no need for anyone to inform Him about us.

Chapter 3
Eternal Life by the Eternal

The chapter contains the best known verse in this Gospel, if not in the entire Bible: *"For God so loved the world, that he gave his only begotten Son, that whosoever believeth in him should not perish, but have everlasting life"*. Chapters 3 and 4 illustrate that the scope of the gospel is the whole world. In chapter 3 we find a prominent Pharisee from Judea and in chapter 4 a woman from Samaria as well as a man from Galilee, v. 42.

The portion reveals the need for a new birth. The learned Nicodemus did not understand the Lord's teaching, even though the Old Testament testifies to the truth of a new birth: "I will give them one heart, and a new spirit will I put within them; I will give them one heart, and a new spirit will I put within them," *Ezek. 11.19, 36.25 to 27.* He thought well of Christ, but not well enough, vv. 2, 13. He progressed from congratulating Him, v. 2, to being converted by Him. We note his desire for Christ, ch. 3; his defense of Him, 7.45 to 52; his devotion to Christ, 19.38 to 42.

The serpent on *the pole, Num. 21:9*, is typical of the great salvation available by faith in Him who was lifted up on the cross. It was necessary for Christ to go to Golgotha; note the imperative of the sinner in v. 7 (it is necessary to be born again), of the Savior in v. 14 (it is necessary to be lifted up) and of the believer in v. 30 (it is necessary for Him to grow). The one who went to the cross was the Son of God and in this He expressed God's love for man, v. 16. A great source of love - God; a great object - the world; a great gift - His Son; a great possibility - whosoever, or *"whosoever"*; a great condition - to believe in Him; a great possession - eternal life.

John is the apostle of the antitheses:

Death and life v. 16

Condemnation and salvation v. 17

Faith and unbelief v. 18

Light and darkness v. 19

Love and loathing v 19, 20

Doing wrong and practicing the truth v 20, 21

The gospel does not know neutrality; men are either for Christ or against him.

John the Baptist gives an eloquent testimony to the Lord and evidences an excellent understanding of his own position in relation to Christ vv 29, 30. He points Christ out to the men and then withdraws. It is possible to proclaim Christ and then hinder those who want to follow him. Not so with John; to the extent that Christ makes himself known, John gladly absents himself.

Chapter 4
El Pozo es Hondo

The woman of Samaria was greatly surprised when the Lord, being a Jew, asked her what to drink. When he then spoke of the water that he could give, she misunderstood, thinking that he meant the water that was in the well. Because he had nothing to draw with, she said, "The well is deep. Of course, this is true in a literal sense, because the well is more than thirty meters deep, but it is more true in a spiritual sense. And, what Christ provides is much more than a deep well; it is a fountain of water springing up to eternal life.

In the conversation thus begun the woman's thoughts ceased to focus on the well, and even on her pitcher, to consider the extraordinary person with whom she was confronted. He made known his knowledge of her past and present life, and revealed the true meaning of worship as well as stating clearly that he was the Messiah.

Many of the Samaritans believed in Him as a result of the woman's testimony, vv 29, 39 to 42. The disciples, too, learned that the Lord was sustained by what is not related to physical need but by doing the will of the Father, v. 34.

The second sign of the Gospel is in this chapter. Again the Lord visited Cana, where He was received by an official of King Herod. He had a seriously ill son in Capernaum, almost fifty kilometers away. Apparently the man thought that Jesus would travel from Cana to Capernaum to heal the boy, but when he found out the man's sincerity, he sent him away because his son was already well. The Lord healed him without seeing him and in this way showed His dominion over distance.

The official expected a slow recovery, but was informed by his servants that the fever was gone altogether, and then the man realized that this had happened just as Jesus gave the word. As a result, the official believed along with his own.

The son had been in a hopeless condition at a distance from Christ, but yet was wonderfully saved by the word of the Lord. The believer also was once in a hopeless condition, ***Ephesians 2:1 to 3***, estranged from Christ, 2:11, 12, but has been saved, 2:4 to 10, 13 to 22.

If the first sign, John 2, was a manifestation of Christ's glory, the second illustrates an absolute trust in Him.

Chapter 5
Christ is Equal with God

The healing of the sick man is the third sign in this Gospel. Chapter 2 presents Christ as the Lord of quality when He changed the water into wine and chapter 4 saw Him as the Lord of distance when He healed the nobleman. The opening of chapter 5 presents him as the Lord of time as 38 years presents no difficulty in healing the man by the pool. Whether the young, 4.46, or the old, 5.5, Christ has the ability to meet the need.

It was on a Sabbath day that the man was healed, and this prompted the Jews to persecute Jesus. When the Lord said, "My Father worketh hitherto, and I work," v. 17, the Jews sought still more to kill Him, not only because in their opinion He had not kept the Sabbath, but because, by referring to God as His own Father, He had made Himself equal with God. He did:

- In work: "The Son can do nothing of himself, but what he sees the Father doing;

For whatever the Father does, the Son does likewise", v. 19.

- In knowledge: "The Father loves the Son, and shows him all things that he does;

and greater works than these will he show him", v. 20.

- In rising from the dead: "As the Father raises the dead and gives them life, even so also the Son to whom he will he gives life", v. 21. Also vv 28, 29.

- In judging: "The Father judges no one, but has given all judgment to the Son", v. 22.

Also v. 27.

- In honoring: "He who does not honor the Son does not honor the Father who sent him." v. 23.
- In regenerating: "He that heareth my word, and believeth on him that sent me, hath everlasting life;

and shall not come into condemnation, but has passed from death unto life", v. 24.

- In his own existence: "As the Father has life in himself, so he has given life to the Father in his own life.

to the Son to have life in himself", v. 26.

The Jews were right in their observations but wrong in their unbelief. The Son did nothing and taught nothing on his own, vv 19, 30, 8.28, 12.49. The only deed he claimed to be his own was that of laying down his own life, 10.18.

Chapter 6.1 to 21
Lord of Quantity and Natural Law

This portion contains two more signs than are included in the Gospel. In chapter 2 we see Christ as the Lord of quality, while here, in the feeding of the five thousand, He is Lord of quantity. The second sign is Christ walking on the water as evidence of being Lord of the natural law.

A great multitude had followed the Lord, and now he wanted to give them something to eat. He asked Philip about this, knowing perfectly well what he intended to do. He did not need Philip's advice, but Philip needed the proof. Philip focused on the vastness of the need, but unfortunately left Christ out of his calculations. Do we? Andrew offered a suggestion but emphasized the smallness of the supply. For Philip it was a question of deciding between the Master and the crowd. Which is greater? For Andrew it was a question of the Master or the boy.

That the Lord was more than adequate to the situation is evident from the fact that He not only satisfied the multitude but also produced a surplus. There is satisfaction and surplus in Christ.

The effect of the miracle on the people was that they resolved to make Jesus king, v. 15. After all, it would be of great benefit to them. For this reason the Lord withdrew to a mountain.

When the sun went down, the disciples went to the Sea of Galilee for the purpose of crossing to Capernaum. It was dark and the sea became restless because of a strong wind. With great effort they rowed about seven kilometers on the lake and then they saw Jesus walking on the water, v. 19. His glory is revealed in that he walks on the waves of the sea, *Job 9.8*, and the darkness is the same as the light, *Psalm 139.12.* We also see his grace in his words of power and peace: "I am he; do not be afraid".

The disciples were frightened, v. 18; troubled, v. 19; but then assured, v. 20. The Lord had been for them on the mountain but now He is with them in their difficulty. He refused the crown of the multitude but made His own see that He was King indeed - the ruler of wind, darkness and sea. Is all this for you?

Chapter 6.22 to 71
Christ the Sustainer of Life

———

Christ had claimed to be the source of life, 5.24 to 26, and in chapter 6 he taught his disciples that he was also the sustainer of life.

We see that most had wrong motives for seeking Jesus. It is not a matter of acting for what is only of passing value, but of believing in the One who can give what is eternal in its nature, v. 27.

The Lord Himself was the true bread from heaven of which the Old Testament manna was a type. Indeed, it is the bread of God. If it satisfies God, is it not more than enough to satisfy us? The Lord claimed to be the bread of life and promised that those who come to Him will never hunger, and by believing in Him they will never thirst.

The full answer to genuine spiritual hunger and thirst is Christ Himself. Do we enjoy being sustained by Him? The Lord promised that if a man eats of the bread from heaven, he will live forever. In fact, He said that unless we eat by faith of the flesh of the Son of God, and so eat of His blood, we cannot have eternal life, vv 51 to 54.

The climax of his teaching is in vv 56, 57: "He who eats my flesh and drinks my blood abides in me, and I in him. As the living Father sent me, and I live because of the Father, so he who eats me will live because of me." Many of the disciples found this teaching offensive and ceased to accompany him. However, Peter made it clear that he truly grasped what Christ meant when he declared, "It is the spirit that gives life; the flesh profits nothing; the words that I have spoken to you are spirit and are life." Peter's response is a high point in the apostle's experience: "Lord, to whom shall we go? You have the words of eternal life.

Jesus not only can satisfy his people, but he is the one who will ultimately glorify them, vv 39, 40. It is certainly a necessary exercise to analyze what we believe, but it is only by a proper appropriation for ourselves of his Person and work that we receive the confidence of eternal blessing. Is ours also Peter's magnificent confession, "We have believed and know that thou art the Christ, the Son of the living God," v. 69. Compare it with another great confession of his in **Matthew 16:16**: *"Thou art the Christ, the Son of the living God."*

Chapter 7
No Man Has Ever Spoken Like This Man

This chapter presents Christ speaking to various groups.

<u>TO HIS BROTHERS</u>: They advised the Lord to go up to the feast of tabernacles to make Himself known to the people. However, he refused to accompany them, saying, "My time has not come, but your time is always ready." Of course, he knew what it would be better to do much more than they knew. We always need his grace to act rightly toward others in our families, especially if we find among them unsaved people.

<u>TO THE JEWS</u>: Subsequently the Lord went to the feast privately. About halfway through the feast, Jesus entered the temple and taught. The Jews considered it a wonderful thing that one should speak as he did, never having learned from the schools of the rabbis. The Lord affirmed: "My doctrine is not mine, but his who sent me. He that will do the will of God, shall know whether the doctrine be of God, or whether I speak of myself." As we marvel at the Lord, may our admiration turn to adoration!

<u>TO THE MULTITUDE</u>: The Lord challenges them about their healing initiative on the Sabbath. If it was permissible to circumcise on the Sabbath, why not the complete restoration He had effected? He concluded with, "Judge not according to appearances, but judge with righteous judgment."

Religion without reality should not be confused with truth expressed by love.

We find more noble words of Christ in vv 28 to 34: "He who sent me is true, whom you do not know. Yet a little while, and I will be with you, and go to him that sent me. Ye shall seek me, and shall not find me." We note especially his words on the last day, that great day of the feast, in vv 37, 38: "If anyone thirsts, let him come to me and drink. He who believes in me... out of his innermost being shall flow rivers of living water." Then he explains: "This he said of the Spirit, which they that believed on him should receive: for the Holy Ghost was not yet come.

There was a division among the people because of Him, and it is ever so. It was the officers who uttered the words that form our heading, when they returned to the chief priests and Pharisees, v. 46. At this juncture Nicodemus came to the defense of Christ, the one who would later express his devotion to Him, 19.39. May our appreciation for the Lord cause us to do what Nicodemus did - defend the validity of the word and express our thanks to Him for having suffered on the cross.

Chapter 8.1 to 11
Full of Grace and Truth

———

The last verse of chapter 7 constitutes rather the first verse of chapter 8. The Lord was always in communion with His Father, a great example for us!

While teaching in the temple, the religious leaders presented him with a woman taken in adultery, and asked him if the woman should be stoned according to *Deuteronomy 22:22*, thus trying to put him on the spot. If on the one hand He were to affirm the validity of the Mosaic law, it would be in effect encouraging an action contrary to Roman law, since the Jewish authorities were not permitted to administer the death penalty. On the other hand, to discard the Levitical law would in effect be to renounce their eagerness to fulfill it. The leaders were well aware of the problem and took full advantage of the opportunity to accuse the Lord.

Jesus bent down and with his finger wrote in the sand. In this way he took his eyes off her, because the accusers were more interested in pointing out other people's sins than in confessing their own. The Lord, therefore, revealed to them the depth of their own sinful nature. His answer in 8.7, "Let him that is without sin among you be the first to cast a stone at her," took the question out of the legal plane and placed it in the spiritual. He made the point that freedom from external guilt is not evidence of being without sin. Would any of those accusers dare to cast the first stone, like those in *Deuteronomy 17:7*?

Again He bowed to the ground, giving the accusers an opportunity to withdraw. Jesus and the woman found themselves alone. His adversaries could not condemn the woman, and Jesus would not. The law could not distinguish between the sinner and her sin; it had to condemn both. But He could distinguish, and so He said to her, "Go, and sin no more." It was made clear that the Lord did not tolerate her sin but neither did He condemn the sinner.

The finger of God had written the law, *Exodus 31:18*, *Deuteronomy 9:10*. He wrote it again that day in the temple. Jesus not only knew it, but had given it its origin. He also knew the hearts of those who confronted him that day. Before them he bowed down and stood up; and, to deal with sin, he died and rose again on the third day.

Chapter 8.12 to 59
The Singular Son of God

The Lord referred to the Father as "my Father", evidencing a unique relationship that existed between Father and Son. We note in the reading "the Father", "a Father", "your Father", but Christ considered Him as His own in a peculiar way. They partake of the same nature. Several times in the chapter he used the expression I am, possessing a character that does not admit of full explanation. Certainly his opponents could not understand it because of their unbelief. How dire the consequences of refusing to believe in Christ.

In view of His unique relationship with His Father, He could claim that He always did what was pleasing to Him and could challenge His accusers as to His sinlessness. Such was his confidence in the fulfillment of the program set before him that men did not fear for him, 8.20, 59. He could even prophesy about the manner of death to which he was to submit, another evidence of his deity.

He referred to his followers as his disciples. They will enter into the fullness of what it means to follow him if they remain at his word, and we are struck by the importance of hearing and keeping his word, v. 31 (you will truly be my disciples), v. 51 (he will never see death), and the effects of resisting it, v. 37 (my word finds no place), v. 43 (you do not understand my language). Do we highly esteem his word? Those whom the Lord describes as "my disciples," not only abide in his word but also love one another, 13.35, and bear fruit, 15.8.

Even though the Pharisees would not accept his testimony, the Lord said, "My testimony is true." He could affirm this because he came from heaven and was going back there. He could also invoke the Father as his witness, vv 14, 18.

The Lord spoke of "my day. It was that day that Abraham had seen long before Jesus was born into this world. Bethlehem was not the beginning of His existence; He could say: "Before Abraham was, I am", v. 58. The wonder of His majestic person impels us to bow before Him and say, "*Bow down to Him, for He is your Lord,*" **Psalm 45:11.**

Chapter 9
Lord Over Misfortune

———

In passing by, the Lord met a man who had been blind from birth. He was a beggar, and projects the image of a sinner, both by nature, *Ephesians 2:3*, and by practice, Romans 3:23. However, the Lord made it clear that the man's physical condition was in no way related to his personal sin or that of his parents.

The Lord who is the light of the world, 8.12, 9.5, gave sight to the blind man. How pleasing it is to observe that it was at his word that the Lord changed water into wine, but anointed the blind man's eyes with mud and sent him to wash in the pool of Siloam. The man could not see the face of the Lord, but he could feel that touch of compassion! He was an unfortunate individual, but he found Jesus to be Lord even of misfortunes.

The aftermath of the miracle reveals the exceptional commotion it caused. John shows that the minds of the people reacted to the healing in different ways. The neighbors showed the curiosity and skepticism that were to be expected. The Pharisees showed their prejudice against Christ, on the grounds that he had healed on a Sabbath day. They opposed the man and tried to force him to submit to their authority, but when all their abuse and threats failed, they threw him out of the synagogue. They said they wanted to honor God, v. 24, and Moses, vv 28, 29, but at the expense of the Lord Jesus Christ. How foolish!

The man's parents do not look good. Afraid of any public sympathy for their son when confronted by the leaders, they adopted a petty neutrality and placed the responsibility on someone else. But, notwithstanding all the opposition, the man's testimony was outstanding. For him, Christ was greater than all his trouble and opposition. He progressed from amazement, v. 25, to worship, v. 38. His development is striking: for him Jesus was a man, v. 11; a prophet, v. 17; the Son of God, v. 38. He had lost the synagogue of the Jews, vv 28, 34, but found the Son of God, vv 35-38.

Chapter 10
The Good Shepherd

This chapter mentions five types of men who relate to sheep.

<u>The stranger, v. 5</u> He could possibly attempt the work of the shepherd but in reality he would be seeking to do what was not his calling. He would approach the sheep in vain and they would not know or trust him. They would flee.

<u>The hireling, v. 12</u> While the stranger could assume functions that are not his own, the hireling has no duty to the flock; the one who works only for pay does have a responsibility, but his character is revealed by the way he performs his function. The sheep flee from the stranger, but the hireling flees from the flock when it needs him most. He does so because what interests him most is the salary, not the flock.

<u>The thief, v. 1</u> He is worse than these other two, because he comes with deliberately evil intentions, v. 10. The hireling sought profit and rendered service while there was no danger to himself. However, the thief sees the flock as prey. We will now look at two more, very different ones.

<u>The doorkeeper, v. 3</u> He personally is not of necessity a shepherd, but can be identified with a true shepherd. John the Baptist was one indeed, but it is to be regretted that there were many who considered themselves shepherds of the flock of Israel and disowned the Good Shepherd when he came, v. 11.

<u>The Shepherd, v. 2</u> Unlike the thief, he does not come to take away but to give, v. 28. Unlike the hireling, he does not sacrifice the sheep

to save himself, but sacrifices himself to save the sheep, v. 11. Unlike the stranger, his voice is known to the sheep, v. 27. They are his and he knows them by name, vv 3, 14.

The Lord Jesus is truly the Good Shepherd who knows his own sheep by name, and they know him. Such is His love for the sheep that He laid down His life for them. In his care they are eternally secure, v. 28. The shepherds in the local church have as their supreme example the Chief Shepherd, *1 Peter 5.2 to 4. He* reminds the undershepherds of the high esteem he has for those whom they care for, as he describes them as "my sheep", v. 27.

Chapter 11
Lord Over Death

———

The miracle of Lazarus' resurrection shows that Christ is Lord even over death. John writes that these signs are recorded so that we may believe that Jesus is the Christ, the Son of God, 20:31.

In our meditations we have seen in Christ's miracles proofs that he is:

Lord of quality by changing water into wine chapter 2

Lord of the distance in healing the nobleman's son chapter 4

Time Lord in healing the man by the pool chapter 5

Lord of quality in feeding the five thousand chapter 6

Lord of natural law walking on the water chapter 6

Lord over misfortune on healing the man born blind chapter 9

Lord of the dead by raising Lazarus from the dead chapter 11

As in chapter 9, John now deals not only with the sign itself, but also with previous events and the aftermath. Before the miracle, upon receiving the message from Mary and Martha about their brother's illness, the Lord stayed two days at the place where he was. That he could have healed Lazarus from a distance, there is no doubt, 4.47 to 54, but he did not and Lazarus died.

The Lord knew of Lazarus' death without being notified; this is another evidence of his deity. Arriving in Bethany, both Martha and Mary felt that Lazarus would not have died if the Lord had been present. We may not always understand his will, but we can always rest in his love. He is too loving to be thoughtless and too wise to err.

After the tremendous affirmation of His being "the resurrection and the life," Martha responds with an excellent confession, vv 25, 27. He was the Son of God, vv 4, 27, but perfectly human also in the midst of anguish. Having prayed, the Lord cried with a loud voice, "Lazarus, come forth." He did so, and wrapped in linen cloths; the Lord gave the command, "Loose him, and let him go." There is life and liberty in Christ.

Chapters 5 to 12 tell of the growing opposition to Christ, and it is at this juncture that it is resolved to kill him.

Chapter 12.1 to 9
Worship and Witness

———

The Lord had the cross very much in mind as He withdrew to Bethlehem. At supper, Mary took a very costly ointment and anointed Jesus' feet. She wiped the feet with her hair and the house was filled with the fragrance of the perfume. Mary's appreciation for Christ was so great that she did not hesitate to anoint Him with what was worth much, and with this others entered into the preciousness of her adoration of Him. And do others share in the value of the fragrance when I adore Him?

Martha worked for Christ, Lazarus ministered to Christ and Mary worshipped Christ. Are these characteristics typical for me? What Mary did was costly, she was criticized and praised. She often found herself at the feet of Christ. In a favorable situation, Luke 10.38 to 41, she sat at his feet and listened to what he said. In *John 11:28 to 32* she prostrated herself before Him in adversity, and in 12:3 she anointed His feet in a mysterious scene that pointed to His sufferings. Mary's example teaches us that when we are in prosperity, or facing adversity, or before a mystery, we must be "at his feet."

Lazarus was a true believer in Christ. He enjoyed fellowship at the supper and was the means of leading others to Christ. Also, he was in danger because of his connection with the Lord, v. 10; compare *2 Timothy 3:12*: *"all who desire to live godly in Christ Jesus will suffer persecution"*.

The passage narrates Christ's triumphal entry into Jerusalem, vv 12, 13, in remarkable humility and in fulfillment of the prophecy of

Zechariah 9:9: *"Behold, your king will come to you, righteous and savior, humble, and riding upon an ass, upon a colt the foal of an ass."* The disciples failed to grasp the full meaning of this on that occasion, but learned the meaning when the Lord was glorified, v. 16. The ascension made them aware of the Lord's sovereignty, and may He do the same in us! Note the retention of "these things" in v. 16.

The section ends with the despair of the leaders, v. 19, who felt that Jesus was gaining popularity. How little they understood God's plan! v. 23.

At that juncture the disciples did not understand the momentous events of those days. It was only by reflecting on them that John came to appreciate the significance of "these things". May we too grow in our appreciation of Christ and his accomplishments.

Chapter 12.20 to 50
We would like to see Jesus

Among those attending the feast were certain Greeks who approached Philip with a view to gaining an interview with Jesus. Their desire was excellent: "Sir, we would like to see Jesus",

As servants of Christ, we should remember what men really need - not good ideas or good advice, but the good news about Jesus! Philip required Andrew's support in approaching Christ; Andrew was always on hand to lead one to Him. He was a true Christian missionary - the first home missionary, 1:41; the first missionary to children, 6:8, 9; the first foreign missionary, vv 21, 22. Andrew always had time and patience to attend to the requests of even children and strangers.

How appropriate that the Lord then spoke to them of the grain of wheat falling into the ground and dying that it might bear much fruit. He spoke to them also of His coming death, which would draw many to Himself, and pointed out how He would die: *"obedient unto death, even death on a cross,"* **Philippians 2:8**. Christ's sovereignty is by His sacrifice. Even in this dark hour, with Jesus' death soon to be realized, John emphasizes once again the essential deity of Christ by pointing out that Isaiah saw His glory and spoke of Him, v. 41; *Isaiah 6.1 to 10.*

The Lord said that to believe in Him was to believe in God, v. 44, and to see Him was to see the One who sent Him,

v. 45, 14.9. He came for the purpose of salvation, but by rejecting Him men reject God and expose themselves to judgment.

One of the great tragedies of human history is recorded in v. 37: "although he had done so many signs before them, they did not believe in him". With all the advantages of proximity, life, hearing, observation and conversation, people did not believe in Him. Later the Lord said, in effect, that seeing is not believing and believing is seeing, 20.29. We thank God that the believer understands this reversal of human judgment on the part of the Lord. Throughout chapters 5 to 12 the Lord's power is questioned, but against that background we see Him as:

The source of life chapter 5

Life Support chapter 6

The source of truth chapter 7

The light source chapters 8 and 9

The source of love chapters 10 to 12

Introduction to the ministry in the upper room

The reference to the Lord's love, 13.1, introduces not only the washing of the feet but the whole section, including the discourses to the end of chapter 16 and the prayer of chapter 17. Christ's loving interest was demonstrated in the visible act of service, and is no less evident in the discourses that follow. We see Him providing for the welfare of the disciples after His departure, preparing them for the bitter blow they were to receive, hiding from them the painful facts about how He would go, providing them with thoughts of His glory and a place in the Father's house, all with a view to supporting them in the crisis they would soon face. All these things, and others, combine to highlight the Lord's love for His own.

"He loved them to the end" means more than that He loved them until the moment of His farewell. He continued to love them at the right hand of the Father. His love does not change, it is eternal. The statement concentrates on the character of love and not on the time factor. The idea is that He loved them to the end, with a love that knew no limitations and even urged Him to wash their feet. In a few hours He would humble Himself even more to the shameful death of crucifixion.

If the words of 14:31, "Arise, let us depart from here" mean that Jesus and his disciples left the upper room at once, it is understood that the speeches that follow and the prayer (chapters 15 to 17) were delivered on the walk to Gethsemane, where they entered after crossing the brook Kidron. The dominant theme is now the world with its ungodliness and hatred, the apostles in the world and the testimony of the Holy Spirit. As far as the Lord was concerned, his words in 14:31, "Arise, let us go from here," show his willingness to go out and meet his persecutors and thus fulfill the will of his Father whom he loved.

These chapters, 13 to 17, begin with the washing and end with intercessory prayer. Together with all that is said between these two ends, they throw valuable light on the ministry of Christ in heaven as our Great High Priest.

Chapter 13.1 to 17
Mr. Kneeling

———

The washing of the disciples' feet was an act of love and service; they are two things closely linked, even to the point of not being able to be separated when they appear in this sequence. It is possible to serve without love, *1 Corinthians 13:1 to 3*, but we cannot love without serving. Love must be expressed in action and always for the good of others. Love is selfless but self is pleased to be served. This was perfectly displayed by the One, into whose hands the Father had committed all things, when He took off His robe, bowed His body and rendered service. All the details of this initiative of love were performed by Himself: He laid aside His garment, took a towel, girded Himself with it, poured water into the basin, washed the feet of others and wiped them.

This ministry is all the more impressive when we consider it against the background of the events that were taking shape and were shortly to take place: the betrayal of Judas, the denial of Peter, the arrest and the trials. The foreknowledge of what was coming upon him must have increased his sorrow, but he was more disturbed by them than by himself, loving them to the end.

However, there was a deeper meaning in what he did. It was not understood at the time, but later it was, when the Spirit came. It was a parable expressed in deed that taught practical sanctification. Christians are cleansed once for all through the work of Christ on the cross, but they need daily washing from defilement as they walk this scene that is the world. Peter protested in the first instance, but he had to submit to Christ or lose fellowship with Him, for there can be no fellowship without cleansing. The water is symbolic of the Word, the means by which washing is effected in believers, ***Ephesians 5:26*** *("having cleansed her by the washing of water by the word")* and in Psalm 119:9 ("Wherewithal shall a young man cleanse his way? By keeping thy word"), and the whole scene is illustrative of the ceaseless ministry which the Lord performs for our good as High Priest in heaven.

The moral lesson is summarized in vv 14, 15: "ye also ought" and "ye also ought to do". The former involves an obligation and the latter an example. To do for others what Jesus did is not only a matter of duty but also because He set the example. To fail to do so is to put ourselves above the One who set the standard. This service will not be done out of censure but in love through the water of the word.

Chapter 13.18 to 38
The Disturbed Host

————

Jesus was troubled in soul in 12:27 and now in 13:21 he is troubled in spirit, the highest sphere of his being. Consequently, the sadness he felt was more intense. The cause was the presence of the betrayer. It was not anger at what Judas was plotting, but anguish because of what the son of perdition was bringing upon himself. When Judas finally left the room, it was of his own free will. However, Judas' perfidy was no surprise to Christ. It was foretold in the Psalms and Jesus knew his character when He chose him, v. 18. His announcement that the traitor was among them must have made Judas blush, but he seems to have given no hint of guilt.

The others did not suspect him, even when he left the premises. They thought he had gone out to shop or to give away, when in fact he had gone out to sell and to receive. In selling to the Lord, he sold himself, and the small sum he received was worth nothing compared to the price he paid spiritually. He went out into the "night," and later into the eternal night.

If the revelation of v. 21 did not stop him in his ruinous path, it produced a different effect on the others and resulted in an examination of heart. The tense atmosphere was established by deeds and not words; even Peter kept silent and beckoned to John. If the Lord's supper was not introduced until after Judas' departure, then the examination of conscience anticipates the exhortation to self-examination in *1 Corinthians 11:28.*

In the absence of Judas, Christ's anguish gives way to thoughts of glory. Christ was glorified in the death of Lazarus, 11.4, but now he will be glorified by his own death. By accepting death because of betrayal ("What you are about to do, do the sooner") the Son of Man attained glory right there at this moment: "Now is the Son of Man glorified." However, the glory of v. 32 was still future, referring to the resurrection that took place without delay: "God ... will at once glorify him." Thoughts of His glory did not make Him forget what He was about to leave behind. They had counted on Him for support, but now they would have to support each other out of love. This, and nothing else, was to mark them as His disciples. Peter wanted to distinguish his discipleship with dying for Christ, but he would soon learn how weak he was and that Christ would first have to die for him.

Chapter 14.1 to 11
Father's House

The themes introduced in this discourse are designed to comfort the troubled disciples. Jesus, troubled in body, 11:33, in soul, 12:27, and in spirit, 13:21, now says to his own: "Let not your heart be troubled." The heart is not only the seat of feeling, but of faith: "with the heart man believeth unto righteousness," Romans 10.10. Now they were to walk by faith, and a troubled heart would leave faith without effect. Alas! their faith was overcome by arrest, trial and crucifixion, but if they had believed in God who arranged all things, and in Christ who came to carry out His will, despair would not have conquered them.

The first game of consolation consists in opening heaven to their faith. They cherished ideas of a place in an earthly kingdom, but He had planned for them something far better, namely, a place in the Father's house above. It was prepared for them, first by the shedding of His blood, and then by the presentation of its value in the Father's presence. Christ had to be absent to ensure his return to take them. By not returning, it would mean that his work on the cross and his presentation before God had failed altogether. For the time being the believer is in Christ, but the purpose of His return is that the believer can be with Christ. To be with Him will involve two considerations: a glorious vision, "that they may see my glory which thou hast given me," 17.24; and a glorious change, *"we shall see him as he is," 1 John 3.2.* What a perspective this is in contrast to that of the unconverted! *John 7.34, 8.21.*

Going to the Father's house is still in the future. In the meantime, however, there can be access to the Father, just as the Lord teaches

Thomas. He said: *"I am the way"*, *not, "I will be the way"*, which means that the entrance to the Father is present and permanent: *"We have access by one Spirit to the Father"*, **Ephesians 2:18**; *"... having liberty to enter into the Holy of Holies"*, **Hebrews 10:19**. For Thomas, knowing the end was essential to knowing the way. However, in matters of faith the first necessity is to know the way; it is to know a Person and not a method; it is to know the truth about the end, v. 7, and also the life by which the end can be reached, and this end is to know the Father.

Philip thought that a vision could do more than three years of ministry by words and deeds on the part of the One who is the revelation of the Father. By way of comparison, a vision could do little; in reality it could do no more than it did for Moses in **Exodus 33:18 to 23**, when he said, *"I pray thee, show me thy glory."*

Chapter 14.12 to 31
Power through Prayer

The Lord pointed to His works as proof of His union with the Father, v. 11; thus, the works of the disciples were to be evidence of their union with Christ. They would perform even greater works, not in power but in scope. The Lord's work was largely confined to Palestine, but the apostles tended a wider ministry, as recounted in Acts. In a sense the works would still be those of the Lord, *Mark 16:20*: *"they... preached everywhere, the Lord helping them"*. The success of the apostles depended on faith, prayer and the Holy Spirit. The importance of the first - *"he that believeth on me,"* *John 14:12* - is perceived by the use of the verb *"believe"* seven times in this chapter.

As to the prayer we read of its scope, "whatsoever ye shall ask;" the condition, "in my name;" and the motive, "that the Father may be glorified in the Son." "In my name" corresponds to the phrase "in Christ" often found in the Epistles, and expresses the sense of union with Him. Where the prayer accords with this bond, there is the assurance of His active cooperation, "I will," v. 13. To ask "in His name" means also to ask in the person of One who is co-equal with the Father, so that the consequence is doubly certain.

The Holy Spirit, who would provide the power, is called "another Comforter," hinting at his divine personality. He takes the place of Christ who had been with the disciples for some three years; however, the Spirit would remain with them and dwell in them always. Far from losing by Christ's absence, they were to gain an additional source of comfort. The word translated here as *"Comforter"* is expressed as

"Advocate" in **1 John 2:1.** It is seen that there is One in heaven and One on earth to plead our cause.

The manifestation made to those who love Christ, 14.21, is not physical but spiritual. It is by the Spirit that communion is enjoyed. He teaches as well as comforts. Jesus taught many things, but the Spirit teaches all things and gives understanding about what Christ said before, v. 26.

In His parting Christ left peace and also gave peace as a possession to be secured for them by His death. Being sinless, neither death nor Satan-who had the power of death-had claim upon Him, who died in love and obedience to His Father, vv 30, 31.

Chapter 15.1 to 27
True Life

———

Christ is the true, authentic vine, in contrast to Israel, which did not bear fruit for God: *"He had hedged it in and broken it up and planted it with choice vines"*, **Isaiah 5:2;** *"You brought a vine out of Egypt"*, **Psalm 80:8.** The disciples, being branches, were then what the nation had ceased to be. The natural vine exists for one purpose only, namely, to bear fruit. It is useless for anything else, even as a nail to support anything, **Ezekiel 15.3.** The disciples were chosen to fulfill this purpose. In v. 2 it is said "in me" of the branch that bears no fruit, thus contemplating the possibility of being a true believer but not bearing fruit. The husbandman, clearly identified in v. 1 as the Father, removes this branch, teaching us the solemn lesson that it would be better not to be left here as a Christian without fruit and without desire to fulfill the function for which he was chosen.

An increase in our fruit depends on pruning and constancy. The farmer is responsible for pruning and the believer for steadfastness. The "more fruit" is a consequence of skillful pruning, that is, the wise discipline that the Father administers, **Hebrews 12.9 to 11.** v. 8 explains that the fruit that awaits, and glorifies Him, is the reproduction of Christ, the vine, in the branches, **Galatians 2.20**, "I no longer live, but Christ lives in me," and 5.22, 23, "the fruit of the Spirit is..." To abide in Him is to allow Him to act in us. In this connection, it is worth noting the pronoun "my":

My words 15.7

My disciples 15.8

My love 15.9

My commandments 15.10

My joy 15.11

My friends 15.14

My name 15.16

The degree of our performance will be a function of the extent to which we allow Christ to be in us.

No longer being of this world would make them the object of the world's hatred. Therefore mutual love would be all the more necessary, vv 12.17. The world loves its own, and with a selfish love, but they should display a self-sacrificing love after the example of the Lord, vv 12,13. There would be persecution against the name they bore, with a view to destroy it, v. 21, *James 2.7, 1 Peter 4.14*. The attitude of the world would be a consequence of ignorance, and for this there was no excuse, vv 22 to 25. Notwithstanding all opposition, they should bear witness for Christ with the help of the Holy Spirit, vv 26,27.

Chapter 16.1 to 11

The Holy Spirit and the World

The abhorrence of the world and the help of the Holy Spirit in witnessing were mentioned in a general way in chapter 16, and are now expounded in greater detail. Persecution of the disciples would take the form of expulsion from the synagogue and violence, even to the extent of being killed. Worse still, this fanaticism would be considered a service to God and permitted in anyone, v. 2. Far from being a manifestation of devotion to God, as these zealous ones imagined, their zeal manifested ignorance of the Father as revealed by Him who was the Son.

The repeated expression, "I have told you these things," points to the way the Lord used to prepare His own in advance for the trials they were to face. For the disciples the main cause of falling would be the reaction of their fellow citizens to their testimony concerning the national hope.

Overwhelmed with sorrow, the disciples failed to appreciate the benefits that would flow from the Lord's absence, or to consider what His farewell would mean to Him. For this reason they did not ask where He was going. He would have to suffer deeper sorrow than theirs before entering into His glory. His ascension was essential to the descent of the Spirit, v. 7, who would convince an unbelieving world. To convince is to lay bare, to confront with evidence, to convict. The Spirit's conviction consists of three elements: sin, holiness and judgment.

Sin has to do with the fallen nature, and the proof is in unbelief, v. 9. Righteousness is not found in the natural man, **Rom. *3.10***, but only in Christ, the proof of which is the ascension, 16.10. Judgment is the inevitable end of sin and the alternative to righteousness, and the proof is the defeat of Satan at the cross, v. 11. It is the work of the Spirit to bring a person to the knowledge that salvation from judgment is in possessing God's righteousness by faith, not by legal obedience. Example of the power of the Spirit's work is seen at Pentecost, ***Acts 2:37-47.***

Chapter 16.12 to 33
The Holy Spirit and the Believer

The "many things" of v. 12 could not be explained to the disciples on that occasion but were taught later by the Holy Spirit. That it was the Lord who spoke to them is confirmed by what is said next about Him; "He will not speak on His own authority", "He will take of mine". In relation to the believer, the work of the Spirit is tripartite:

- He guides into all truth and reveals the glory of Christ, vv 13, 14;

- He manifests what is going to happen, v. 13.

- The Spirit "leads," involving a willingness on the part of the believer to be led.

This direction is to the truth-all of it, and not part of it-as the sphere in which the Christian must walk. Knowing the truth is not enough, *3 John 4.* The way the Spirit glorifies Christ is to make him known. The expression "will make known" at the end of vv 13, 14 means to declare. Where there is a desire to know the Lord, the Spirit actively responds to satisfy it. John's revelation, "the Revelation," cannot be excluded from the things to come that would be set forth, since future events are recorded beginning in chapter 4 of that book.

"Yet a little while" was on the Lord's lips twice. In v. 17 the disciples were perplexed; He repeats in v. 18. In the first "yet a little while" they still saw Him physically, but this lapse ended with His death. The second "a little while" extended to His resurrection and ascension when they were to see Him spiritually, transforming their cause of sorrow into a means of joy. The birth pangs of sorrow would give birth to the joy of a new experience that no one could take away from them.

That rejoicing would be amplified by yet another blessing, that of answered prayer. On the day of Pentecost it would no longer be necessary to speak in allegories; the disciples would have a spiritual understanding of the Father, giving them greater boldness in prayer.

The statement in v. 29 was said in ignorance, "now you speak plainly," and the confession in v. 30 made their ignorance evident. Jesus said, "I came forth from the Father," making known His divine nature; they said, "you have come forth from God," hinting only at a divine mission. Their being scattered proved the weakness of their understanding, but, notwithstanding their failure, the Lord assures them of his own triumph.

Chapter 17
The Lord's Prayer

———

There are many occasions when the Lord prayed without it being revealed to us what He said. There are also a few cases where short prayers are recorded:

Father, I thank you for having heard me, *John 11:41, 42*

Father, glorify your name. *John 12.27, 28*

I praise you, Father, Lord of heaven and earth... *Matthew 11.25, 26*

But the entire content of this sentence has been preserved.

Its meaning is seen in that it crowns the teaching he has just given. "These things," v. 1, refers to what has preceded and not to what comes next. The prayer was also evidence to the disciples of the work as High Priest which He was about to undertake in heaven for their sakes. His words spoken with a loud voice were intended to give joy, v. 13.

The scope of the prayer is seen in that it embraces divine revelation through the Son, vv 1 to 5; the apostles, vv 6 to 19; and the Church, vv 20 to 26. It begins with a reference to Christ's intrinsic and eternal glory, a glory he retained in his humanity, v 5, and ends with mention of his acquired glory, shared with them and contemplated by theirs, v 22, 24.

"That they may be one," v. 11, is the substance of the intercession. The unity of believers and its visible effect on the world is affirmed in v. 21. Christ prays for unity in holiness by asking that they be kept from evil,

vv. 15, 17. While he was here, he kept them safe, v. 12. He also asks for unity in glory, v. 22, in love, v. 23, and in place also, v. 24.

The objects of the Lord's exercise are clearly specified in v. 9. Seven times in the passage they are referred to as given to Christ. They were his by creation but were given to Christ by foreknowledge and election, v. 6.

The style is characterized by a holy reverence: Father, v. 5; holy Father, v. 11; righteous Father, v. 25. He never addressed God as "our Father" because His quality as Son was unique. He enjoyed an intimacy with the Father in equality with Him, and "lifting up his eyes to heaven",

v. 1, makes it known that the spiritual world was never far from the Lord. "Holy Father" is in contrast to the unholy world where he was going to leave his beloved, with all the defilements that would threaten them. "Righteous Father" is in contrast to the iniquity of the world that did not know God and rejected Christ.

Chapter 18
Betrayal, Detention and Trials

The Gospel according to John has been called the spiritual Gospel. John narrates facts that are revelations of spiritual truths, something that is seen even in his account of the passion. One of the characteristics of the burnt offering, *Leviticus 1*, was that of being a voluntary offering, portraying Christ offering himself without blemish to God, *Hebrews 9:14*. It is this aspect that John presents in his account. The reason for the Lord going to the garden was that Judas "knew that place", not to hide but to make himself accessible to be arrested.

He knew that the events ahead were in accordance with the divine plan and therefore "went ahead" of his enemies. Twice He says, "I am"; the first time to identify Himself and the second time to urge them to proceed with their mission, which He could not do without their consent, and to ensure a safe departure for His disciples.

Peter's rebuke, the mention of the cup, and the statement to Pilate - all these show the voluntary character of Christ's sufferings. In view of these things, there was no need to bind Him, as was done in vv 12 and 24.

It seems that Peter's denials took place while the trials before Annas and Caiaphas were in progress, vv. 12-27. Had Peter accompanied John to the judgment seat instead of wandering outside with the antagonistic crowd, he would not have been disturbed. Meanwhile, inside, the Lord was being questioned about his disciples and their teaching, v. 19. His answer focused on his teaching and not on his disciples, most of whom had already fled and one of whom was outside denying him. John was present at the trial and remained faithful to the end.

The civil trial before Pilate began in v. 28 and ended in 19:16. The majesty of the Person of Christ dominates the scene. The real person under examination is not Christ but Pilate, whose spiritual indifference and moral weakness are exposed. The religious hypocrites who refused to enter Pilate's precincts because the Passover feast was about to begin, were ignorant of their own inner defilement of heart that cried out for the death of the sinless Lord. They had no scruples in choosing a thief instead of the One who did no wrong, *Isaiah 53:9.*

Chapter 19.1 to 16
Pilate's Dilemma

———

The civil trial, alternating from outside and inside the courtroom, reflects Pilate's dilemma. Outside, he tries to acquiesce to the Jewish leaders without giving them what they demand. Inside, he is confronted by Christ who reaches his conscience but to whom he is also unwilling to yield. Lacking moral courage, he seeks a middle way out. He decides to offer Jesus to the people as an alternative to a nefarious criminal, thus appealing to their sense of justice. The scheme fails when they opt for Barabbas, 18.40.

Scourging on the part of the soldiers is another attempt to achieve their end, calculated to arouse pity. After Jesus had been the object of play by Pilate's soldiers, it must have been a touching scene to which he addresses the crowd with the words, "Behold the man". To have submitted the innocent Lord to be scourged shows that he, no less than the Jews, has little interest in doing justice. Their aspiration is frustrated; instead of feeling pity, they cry out, "Crucify him, crucify him!" Scourging was only a half-hearted initiative; they insist on the ultimate penalty.

Scoffing, Pilate assigns to them the responsibility of crucifying him. They reply that, contrary to the declarations of Christ's innocence, their law condemns Him to death because "He made Himself the Son of God," and therefore, permission being given, they are willing to execute the judgment, vv 6, 7. Being responsible for the indignities imposed by the soldiers, Pilate, notwithstanding all his ungodliness, has much cause to be disturbed on hearing this additional accusation. He asks

Jesus what his origin is but receives no answer, because the answer given to his previous question had been met with scorn, 18.33 to 38.

Pilate's power over Jesus was not as absolute as he thought; he had to answer to a higher authority, vv. 10, 11. *"There is no authority except from God, and those that exist have been established by God"*, **Romans 13.1.** As a representative of the civil power, he does not act properly and in the end puts Caesar before God and delivers Jesus to be crucified. Caiaphas, however, as a representative of the theocracy, had committed the greater sin. He, more than anyone else, should have recognized the Christ.

"Princes shall take counsel together against the LORD and against his anointed," *Psalm 2.2.*

Chapter 19.17 to 42
The Crucifixion

The details of the crucifixion peculiar to John's account are sobering. "He carrying his cross, went forth," emphasizes the voluntary character of his death. As in the garden he "went forth" to meet his enemies, 18.1, so now he leaves the city and proceeds to Golgotha. The exhortation of **Hebrews 13:13**, *"let us go out to him ... bearing his reproach,"* reminds us what our voluntary response should be.

It is John who tells us that Jesus was crucified with two, "one on either side," v. 18. Even in the scene of his rejection, he occupied the preeminent place.

Only in this Gospel we are told that Pilate drew up the title and refused to change it at the request of the Jews. The Jews had given their allegiance to Caesar and therefore had to submit to the representative of Rome. John informs us that Jesus' undergarment was "seamless," and that it came to be possessed by one of the soldiers, an illustration of the imputed righteousness that clothes the believer. John calls attention to the devout women who, in sharp contrast to the uncouth soldiers who sat and watched, were standing there, including the mother of Jesus. Being the eldest of the sons, Jesus fulfilled his responsibility for Mary's welfare by entrusting her to John.

In response to the fifth cry from the cross, "I thirst," we have the only gesture of mercy extended to the Lord, its inclusion being an indication of John's tenderness. The loud call recorded by the other writers is presented by John as the cry of triumph: "It is finished." He observes that He bowed His head who had found no place to lie down in this world, but at last found rest in the Father to whom He committed the spirit, v. 30.

It is only John who makes it clear that the legs were not broken and that the side was pierced, and shows that these details fulfilled the Scriptures, vv 31 to 37. The one fulfilled the law, *Exodus 12:46* ("neither shall ye break his bone"), *Numbers 9:12*, and the other the prophets, *Zechariah 12:10* ("they shall look upon me whom they have pierced"). All four evangelists make mention of Joseph, but only John adds that he was a secret disciple and that Nicodemus collaborated with him, one whose first meeting had been at night. Both men found new courage and openly identified with Christ, vv 38-42.

Chapter 20

The Resurrection

———

John chooses four cases to show the different ways in which the resurrection was made to be believed in. The first example is John himself, who was the first to arrive at the tomb,

v. 4, although the second to enter. Peter entered first and beheld the careful arrangement of the linens, evidence that the body had not been stolen. John, on entering, grasped the vast significance of what he saw and he believed, v. 8, which is not said of Peter.

For John, the linens were a sign of the resurrection. If the disciples had known the scripture (possibly **Psalm 16:10**, *"Thou shalt not leave my soul in Sheol..."*), the resurrection would not have been a surprise, but the realization of an expected fact, v. 9. For John, at least, it was at this moment a matter of faith, but soon after it would be a fact to be revealed by the Lord Himself.

The next example is Mary, who had been delivered from seven demons, **Luke 8:2**. She was not only the first person to hear the news of the open tomb, but also to see the risen Lord. The love that kept her at the cross to witness the horrific scenes of Calvary, was also the love that kept her at the tomb, where tears evidenced her deep sorrow. The presence of angels must have given confidence that nothing untoward could happen to the body thus cared for *("he shall give his angels charge over thee, to keep thee in all thy ways"*, **Psalm 91:11**), but her anguish could not be appeased except by the One she called "my Lord". Such devotion could not go unrewarded; the would-be gardener called her by name and instantly she knew who he was, just as every sheep knows the voice of the shepherd, 10.3, 4.

The third case occurred in the evening, when the Lord came and stood in the midst of the disciples gathered behind closed doors. The resurrection was proved by the hands and feet shown to them. John mentions the side, and not the feet, because of the deep impression he received as an eyewitness of the piercing of that body.

The last example is Thomas, who was present when Jesus manifested himself again a week later. He was made to believe by being given the opportunity to take a test based on precisely the conditions he proposed. The confession, "My Lord, and my God," is the pinnacle of faith and expresses the proposed goal of the entire Gospel of John, vv 28-31.

Chapter 21
The Epilogue

———

John has stated that his purpose in writing is to lead people to believe in the divine Christ, 20:30, 31. To achieve this end, he chose eight of the miracles that the Lord did, the last of them recorded in 21:1-14. They are all demonstrations of Deity and, because Jesus is the Christ, they project the messianic kingdom.

Moreover, they contain lessons about eternal life. On the occasion of the first miracle, Jesus manifested his glory by turning water into wine; now in resurrection he manifests himself by the success of the catch. John perceives that the stranger on the beach is the Lord, and Peter's reaction was a consequence of John's comment rather than a recognition of his own.

In connection with the character of the Lord as the Messiah, we note here that the Lake of Galilee is called the Lake of Tiberias, after Caesar Tiberius, and is a figure of the Gentile nations from which there will be a great "harvest" for millennial blessing. As for teaching about eternal life, we learn that it is a life of service. Peter's own initiative to go fishing, and his influence on others, proved fruitless, but there were results when the Lord blessed the project. The Lord's presence on the beach, the fish brought ashore and the counting of the fish all foreshadow the review of our service at the judgment seat of Christ.

Peter's restoration, narrated next, brings out the conditions that support service, namely, love for Christ, vv 15 to 17, and surrender to the Lord's will, vv 18, 19. Three times the Lord asks him, "Do you love me?", corresponding to Peter's three denials. The first question questioned his love in comparison with others, "More than these?"; the second, his love for the Lord no more; and the third, the reality of his service. Peter, being informed of his martyrdom, asks about John. The answer given is a reminder of the Lord's sovereignty over his servants. John's service was of no concern to Peter, vv 20 to 22. The Lord who directs our service, vv 1 to 14, and demands our affection, vv 15 to 17, is at the same time the one who determines our destiny, vv 18 to 25.

We cannot know the contents of the infinite number of books that could be written about that holy life, v. 25, but the Father knows, keeping precious memories for eternal ages.

Six Jars in the Gospel of John

"There were six stone water jars there....

Jesus said to them, "Fill these jars", John 2.6.7.

The Scriptures employ vessels as figures of persons. For example, "We have this treasure in earthen vessels, that the excellency of the power may be of God, and not of us."

2 Corinthians 4.7. Paul was a chosen vessel (instrument), Acts 9.15. The number six suggests an application, for in the Bible six is the number of the world in the moral sense, just as four is the number of the world in the quantitative sense. It is perceived, then, that these six vessels may be typical of individuals, and they in turn typical of the condition of the human race.

This is seen to be the case when considering six persons mentioned in the following chapters of John. Each one met Jesus and He dealt with each one according to his respective condition. These six persons are: Nicodemus, the Samaritan woman, the paralytic, the adulteress, the man born blind, and Lazarus of Bethany.

(a) Nicodemus, John 3;

Representative of the religious sinner

The difference between the first two persons is so marked on the moral plane that it lends itself to contrast, but only from the human point of view. There is no difference, according to Romans 3:22, 23. The respected Pharisee of John 3 was as much a lost sinner as was the rejected Samaritan of John 4.

The introductory comment of Nicodemus, Rabbi, indicates that he did not think he was empty. Many thousands have erred in the same way, thinking that they can save themselves, or at least contribute to the enterprise. But if one does not become like a child, he will in no way enter the kingdom. A child is not justified with, "We know".

Therefore, Jesus does not answer him directly, but introduces a new subject. Unless one is born again, he cannot see the kingdom of God. Whatever Nicodemus knew, this was beyond his comprehension. Now he wants to know how one is born old, and he hears that it is by water and the Spirit. Desperate, he asks how this can be. Not to understand these things was unforgivable for a leader among the Jews, and well deserved the rebuke, "Art thou a teacher of Israel, and knowest not this?" Was he unaware of the prophecy of Ezekiel 37 about the dry bones in the valley receiving the breath of life?

The rebuke took effect, and now the Lord proceeds to fill the jar He had emptied. As Moses lifted up the serpent according to Numbers 21, so the Son of Man was to be lifted up, that one might have eternal life by believing in Him. It was the beginning of a new day for Nicodemus. If anyone is in Christ, he is a new creature, or new creation, 2 Corinthians 5.17. Everything is made new, which he evidenced by his attitude in John 7:50 in defending Jesus before the Sanhedrin. This is seen more clearly in John 19, when Nicodemus goes to the Cross and sees the One who satisfied the longings of his soul that unforgettable night, lifted up.

(b) The Samaritan woman, John 4;

Representative of the abandoned sinner

Very significant are the words of 4.4: "it was necessary for him to pass through Samaria". The Savior is eager to converse alone with a Samaritan woman. He waits for her at the well, and we are reminded of

2 Peter 3:9: "The Lord is longsuffering toward us, not willing that any should perish."

With full knowledge of his soul's thirst, he asks for water from the woman, who was unprepared for such a request. The pride in his heart comes to light, as does the supposed superiority of his religion. She did not know who was speaking to her, and could not see beyond the well of her village. In patient grace, Jesus makes her see that the springs of this world are exhausted, but that there is an inexhaustible source of eternal life, and that source is Himself.

Unable to answer Him, the woman defends herself with prophetic truth, but does so in such a way as to imply that she does not trust what He is saying. "The Messiah is to come...he...will declare all things to us." It is precisely the kind of difficulty presented in Nicodemus; namely, a heart occupied with religious criteria but in a way no more. "Teacher of the unlearned, teacher of babes, who hast in the law the form of knowledge and truth," Romans 2.20. Unconsciously she leaves herself exposed to the penetrating sword of the Spirit, and it enters her where she least expected. "I am he that speaketh with thee." And now what were the pitchers and fountains of this world, before the Fountain that offers the heavenly flow? Well forgotten, the woman runs to tell others of her great discovery. Truly, the water of life in her was leaping to eternal life.

I am. For this formerly abandoned sinner, these were the words that brought her salvation. Said later in 18.5, they would be of conviction, to such an extent that armed men would fall to the ground.

(c) The paralytic, John 5;

Representative of the incapacitated sinner

In John 5 the scene changes from the well of Sychar to one of the walls of Jerusalem, namely, the Sheep Gate mentioned in Nehemiah 3:1.

There was a pool there by the name of Bethesda, meaning 'House of Benevolence', which had five porches filled with handicapped people.

It was here that the divine benevolence rested in a striking manner upon the house of Israel, for an angel descended at a certain time of the year and stirred up the waters. On these occasions the first to enter the pool was healed of his disease. We can well imagine how they would all strive to enter. But out of that crowd, only one could be healed each year. They would come with great hope, only to leave sad. And, in our times there are thousands who wait for the moving of the waters, but a vain hope characterizes the religion of many. "Peace with God, I sought to win it with feverish solicitude, but my 'meritorious works' did not give me health."

People are encouraged by false hopes in our day, just as they were, for fallen human nature has not changed over the centuries. If the question that Jesus put to the protagonist of our story had been put before each one in that crowd, perhaps no one else would have been able to answer as he did: "Lord, I have not. Each one would have protested that his chances were as good as anyone else's. But there was one there who had spent the money he had earned. But there was one there who had spent thirty-eight years in waiting, and was still exactly where he started.

There are several ways in which the pool of Bethesda points to the person and work of the Lord Jesus Christ, but we will mention only one or two.

The five porticos stand out. The number five is always associated in the Bible with the claims of God, and there has been only One who can answer His justice. Just as troubled water signifies the Cross, one reflects on the Suffering Holy One of Psalm 69 and its counterpart in John 12.27: "Now is my soul troubled; and what shall I say?"

Like the paralytic, the lost sinner has only to approach the pool, for the movement of the water is the strange work of the Holy Spirit in convicting and presenting the Gospel. To be without Christ is to be without hope, Ephesians 2:12, 1 Thessalonians 4:13. And, in the Bible a forty year time frame is the period of evaluation of the human race, so this man was near his last chance. He was in despair. "At last in despair, 'I can no longer,' I said. And from heaven I heard an answer, 'It is finished.'"

This man was indeed an empty jar. "While I go, another goes down before me." But the grace of the Lord intervened and filled the poor man with not only bodily but also spiritual health: "You are healed; sin no more.

(d) The adulteress, John 8;

Representative of the condemned sinner

There are certain portions of the Word of God that some teachers and preachers claim should not have been incorporated, while others go so far as to say that the Book would be better without them. One such portion consists of the first eleven verses of John chapter 8, in which we read of the encounter with the fourth of the series of individuals in this Gospel whose lives were transformed. Every word of God is pure, and we can be confident that each one has been purified seven times. A distorted imagination can misinterpret the most sublime account, whereas to the pure all things are pure and to the corrupt and unbelieving nothing is pure, Titus 1.15.

Without this story there would be a missing link in the chain we are studying. John 7 ends with a division: each went home, but Jesus went to the Mount of Olives. In the morning he returned to the temple courts. The Pharisees brought to him a woman who had been caught in the act of adultery, so that he might pronounce judgment against her.

He thought he was counting on a trap that would discredit the Master altogether. He would have to acknowledge the terrible penalty that the law of Moses demanded, or declare himself a heretic. "In the law Moses commanded us to stone such women. Thou, then, what sayest thou?"

He did not answer. The Obedient One was fulfilling Ecclesiastes 3:7: "A time to be silent, and a time to speak." But he bowed, as if he had not heard, and with his finger wrote on the ground. They persisted, thinking no doubt that they had cornered him and content in anticipation of their defeat. But he straightened up and said to them, "Let him who is without sin be the first to cast the stone against it." Having said this, he bowed again and wrote.

Isaiah 9:6 speaks of two of his dejections: the Child is born to us and the Son is given to us. He was cast down - "bowed down" - when He was born as a child in Bethlehem and wrapped in swaddling clothes. He "bowed down" again on Golgotha, as a Son given in sacrifice. Both the incarnation and the crucifixion were essential for the guilty sinner to be justified before his Holy God. As for writing on the ground, we read in Jeremiah 17:13: "O LORD, the hope of Israel, all they that forsake thee shall be ashamed; and they that depart from me shall be written in the dust, because they have forsaken the LORD, the fountain of living waters". A name written in the ground does not remain for long. It is soon blotted out by the breath of the four winds of heaven and trodden under foot of men. The names of the saved, on the other hand, are inscribed in the Book of Life, Philippians 4:3, and so that they will never be blotted out, Luke 11:20.

He wrote with the finger, and "the finger of God" is a term employed as an equivalent of the Spirit of God in Matthew 12:28, where it is a parallel event. Nearly twenty centuries have elapsed since God added to his Word by direct revelation, but this silence in no way indicates that he has ceased to be interested in the affairs of his creatures. The Holy

Spirit has been active throughout the whole span, performing one work for the world and another for believers. The first is to convict of sin, righteousness and judgment.

Those who came forward for the purpose of convincing the woman of sin, came out convicted themselves. They departed, the eldest at the head of the shameful line, and the youngest last. This is the order of judgment that grace reverses: "They shall all know me, from the least to the greatest of them," Hebrews 8:11. The woman is left alone in the presence of Jesus, and He asks her, "Woman, where are those who accused you? None of them condemned you?" The answer is short and humble: "None, Lord." And with this the definitive sentence, expression of divine grace and at the same time commandment of the one who filled this jar of new life: "Neither do I condemn you; go, and sin no more".

The accusatory question that a certain apostle throws at the Jews in general is: "You who teach another, do you not teach yourself?" Romans 2:21. The Law in the hands of a sinner is a dangerous weapon, for it becomes a double-edged sword. It turned against these lords for their own discomfort. On one occasion the Lord said that He had not come to abolish the law or the prophets, but to fulfill, Matt. 5.17. Centuries before it had been written of Him that Jehovah was pleased for the sake of His righteousness to magnify the Law and magnify it, Isaiah 42.21, and He does so by removing the guilt from the outward act and placing it upon the inward motive. While He will let the Law do all its work to convince of sin, at the same time He also shows that, by humbling Himself even to the death of the cross, He has a perfect right to save the sinner from the penalty of that very sin. Thus it is that God is just and justifies the one who believes in Jesus, Romans 3:26.

(e) The man born blind, John 9;

Representative of the blind sinner

That there is method in the arrangement of these six incidents, there is no reasonable doubt. But at the same time there are links between them. One male and one female, twice; then two males. In typical Scriptural usage, the male is representative of the intellect and the female of the affections. An intelligent understanding of the new birth, which was presented to Nicodemus, must precede the exercise of the affections in any act of worship, which was presented to the Samaritan woman.

The tragedy of the case today is that many people think they can offer worship to God apart from the new birth and without the Great High Priest as an intermediary. In most cases the affections alone come into play, and affectionate expressions are offered instead of the worship of those who "in spirit we serve God and glory in Christ Jesus, not having confidence in the flesh," Philippians 3:3. Feelings take the place of spirituality, and room is found for the glorification of man. It is lost sight of that God demands what is worship in Spirit and according to Truth.

The command of 5.8, "Arise...walk," makes it clear that an intelligent use of God's Word must control the walk before the affections can respond to the command, "Sin no more," 8.11.

But in the remaining cases there is no room for affections; we enter the sphere of Christ's lordship. It is now a matter of carrying out the commandments of Him whom God has made Lord. There is a marked difference in the way he works in the fifth case and the sixth. He does not merely talk the talk, as before. He has a purpose to fulfill and desires others to know something of what it means.

"Behold what manner of love," says the apostle in 1 John 3:1, and here we find something of his style. It has always been his manner to take from the weak and foolish of this world to confound the wise, so that in John 9 he spits on the ground, makes mud with the spittle, and smears the eyes of the blind man. Having done this, he sends him to the pool of Siloam to wash.

The subject was washed and came back healthy of sight. And the command is still in force: "Anoint thine eyes with eyesalve, that thou mayest see," Rev. 3:18. This is in contrast to Jezebel, who applied the powder of almond shells to the eyes to give a seductive expression to her face, 2 Kings 9.30. But the practices and wiles of that Jezebel woman are not of God. The popular religions of these times recognize the god of this age and do his bidding. This man was a member of the synagogue, but born blind. Many communicants of our generation will protest: "We have eaten and drunk before thee, and thou hast taught in our streets," Luke 13:25-30.

It is therefore with rejoicing that we sometimes find cases like the example in John 9, namely, one who recognizes his condition through the power of the Word of God. The Son of Man came to seek and to save that which was lost, and it is not to be feared that He will overlook such a person. Wherever a sinner recognizes his condition and becomes convinced of his inability to remedy it, he is a sure candidate for God's salvation. The Savior applies the mud and thus appears to intensify the blindness but prevents nature from intervening in any way to change the condition.

"Wash." Washing in the New Testament is always a figure of the experiential cleansing of the way of being by the operation of the Word of God.

The path of obedience leads to suffering. It is noticeable in the Epistles of Peter that obedience and suffering are linked in the text, and so it must always be when God's rights are recognized in a world that opposes him. This man of John 9 hardly recognizes the Lord who gave him his sight, when he finds himself in conflict with the powers of darkness, represented in the scribes and Pharisees. The religion of this world bore the primary responsibility for the crucifixion of the Son of God, as we deduce from the fact that his title was written in Hebrew, Greek and Latin, as a mute testimony to the fact that the religion, culture and power of this world united to kill him.

"And they cast him out." Now the new believer finds himself excommunicated. "They shall put you out of the synagogues: and the hour cometh, when whosoever killeth you shall think that he doeth God service," John 16:2. The Lord also warns, "Blessed are ye, when men shall revile you, and persecute you, and shall say all manner of evil against you, lying. Rejoice and be glad, for your reward is great in heaven; for so persecuted they the prophets which were before you," Matthew 5:11, 12.

It is in this place of rejection that the Lord meets the man to whom he had given his sight, and asks him, "Do you believe in the Son of God?" The man had not yet seen the Lord, though he had heard His voice. "Who is he, Lord?" And when the Lord reveals himself, immediately the man falls at his feet and worships.

Where? Not in the temple, but in the place without name, reminding us of the way Jesus answered the question of 1:38: "Rabbi, where dwellest thou?" His answer on that occasion was: "Come and see", implying that it was a place without name. Let us remember that in Exodus 33:7, the tent was pitched far outside the camp. To have fellowship with the Lord, we must go outside the camp, bearing His reproach, Hebrews 13:13. It is the place of testimony now, the place where His face is seen, where He rules, and where He is acknowledged Lord.

(f) Lazarus, chapter 11;

Representative of the dead sinner

Lazarus is the Greek form of the Hebrew name Eliezer; its meaning is 'God my Helper'. Two men in the New Testament bear this name. At first glance the name does not seem to apply, but both received help from God when they needed it most.

There is little difficulty in tracing from the case of Lazarus of Bethany a comparison of broad application, since the various steps in the story find a parallel in Ephesians 2 where the condition of the unconverted is spoken of. "Behold, he whom thou lovest is sick." And so Ephesians affirms that God had "great love wherewith he loved us," even when we were dead in sins.

This correspondence of ideas is more than a coincidence. It is said that the Lord, having heard the news, did not hasten to the bedside in Bethany, but stayed two days where he was. When he set out on his journey, it took him two days to reach where Lazarus was.

When he arrived, he received the news that Lazarus had been dead for four days. Four of God's days had elapsed when the Lord Jesus manifested "his time" in this world:

When the fullness of time came, God sent his Son, Galatians 4.4

While we were yet without strength, in due time he died for the ungodly, Romans 5.6

With the Lord one day is as a thousand years, and a thousand years as one day, 2 Peter 3.8

It was on the fourth day that the sun was made the center of light. The light had existed, but without being located. In the same vein, the psalmist said that God placed in the heavens a tabernacle for the sun, Psalm 19:9. In John 8 we read of Jesus in the temple court early in the morning and announcing that he was the light of the world.

Martha said, "Lord, if you had been here, my brother would not have died". This is always the reasoning of the human heart. Prevention is thought better than solution, but the divine thoughts are not the human ones, Isaiah 55:8. Why did God allow sin and its consequences, being in a position to have prevented it from happening? He does not always answer our questions, but He does point us to the remedy. On that occasion in the wilderness, when the Israelites were bitten by serpents, he provided the bronze serpent. The remedy was there and the responsibility of each one was to take advantage of it.

Could not this Man who opened the eyes of the blind man have intervened to save the life of Lazarus? 11:37. Yes, he could, but it was not his purpose, nor is it so that he works. The man was created upright, but soon manifested that his innocence was no guarantee against sin. But God introduced a new way, that of redemption and resurrection. "I am the resurrection and the life: he that believeth in me, though he were dead, yet shall he live. And whoever lives and believes in me shall never die forever," 11.25, 26. And the question, "Do you believe this?" Some believers will sleep in Jesus, but there will be at least one generation that will experientially attest to this claim, for we will never sleep. We who are left shall be caught up in the clouds to meet the Lord in the air, and so shall ever be with Him; 1 Corinthians 15.51, 1 Thessalonians 4.16.

Before the tomb, he commands: "Take away the stone". The application is to us believers, since, by the way we walk, we are apt to be a stone of stumbling to the unsaved. May we know how to roll away the stone and walk wisely for those without, so that we may not be a stumbling block, "neither to Jews, nor to Gentiles, nor to the church God," 1 Corinthians 10:32. Now, the freedom of Lazarus is a figure of two truths in John; namely: (1) "If he shall make you free, ye shall be free indeed", 8.36. (2) "Ye shall know the truth, and the truth shall make you free", 8.32.

With the stain of human tears still on the face of the Son of Man, the voice of the Son of God is heard, "Lazarus, come forth!" He was alive, but, as a first step in his freedom, it was necessary to remove the cloths that bound him. Bound head, feet and hands, he could not walk, hear the Lord, nor serve him.

We see in this first stage an illustration of the baptism of the new believer, the first of the two ordinances for the believers of this dispensation. It is a symbol of identification with the death, burial and resurrection of the Lord Jesus Christ. It precedes other steps in the development of the believer; he who has not obeyed by taking this step, does not enter into the full freedom of devotion and service that the Lord desires for His own, although we are not saying that one in this condition cannot shine in personal testimony.

Another example is the account of Israel's experience as given in Hebrews 11:29,30: "By faith they passed through the Red Sea...by faith the walls of Jericho fell down after they had compassed them about seven days." God takes no note of the forty-year interval when they did not walk by faith. He gives them full credit for the fall of Jericho, once they crossed the Jordan, but does not acknowledge in Hebrews how much they had done before.

The command given in Matthew 28:19, 20 is to make disciples (through evangelism), baptize and teach. This teaching will lead to an even greater freedom, which is worship at the Lord's Supper. The blind man who received his sight in chapter 9 took his place outside, in separation, 9:35, "and worshiped". But the case of Lazarus is better; he took his place inside, as a worshipper in close communion with his Lord.

This picture at the beginning of John 12 offers a beautiful illustration of worship. "Six days before the Passover, Jesus came to Bethany." This would be the 9th day of the month, since the Passover was celebrated on the 15th. ("Passover" here, as elsewhere, refers to the feast of unleavened bread. See Luke 22.1). But, in 12.12 "Jesus was coming to Jerusalem." In this way he fulfilled Exodus 12.3, where the Passover lamb is commanded to be taken on the 10th day of the month. We see in John 12 the true Lamb of God "taken" on the tenth day.

(g) Jesus Christ:

A seventh pitcher

It would not be appropriate to end without referring to another jar, or vessel, that was emptied and then filled. It does not appear in the series of six we have studied, but in Philippians chapter 2.

The voluntary humiliation of Christ Jesus, from glory to the cross, is described in seven steps: he did not consider equality with God a thing to be grasped; he emptied himself; he took the form of a servant; he was made in the likeness of men; he humbled himself; he became obedient unto death; and death on a cross. "He emptied himself", 2.7, is translated "he emptied himself" in some versions of the Scriptures. That is, he reduced himself to nothing.

It was necessary to do so in order to redeem fallen man. But the first consequence is another; namely, God also exalted him to the highest place, and gave him a name which is above every name, that at the name of Jesus every knee should bow, of things in heaven, and things in earth, and things under the earth, 2.9.10.

The language in Romans 14:11 is similar but different: "Every knee shall bow to me, and every tongue shall confess to God. What is certain is that the heavenly, earthly and infernal will have to acknowledge the authority of the One who emptied Himself, made Himself anonymous, and gave Himself for the glory of God the Father. The command of the Holy Spirit in Psalm 2:12 is categorical: "Honor the Son, lest he be angry, and you perish from the way.

The Course of a Soul in John 4

Many years now, and many miles from our shores, a small band of men have been spotted early one spring morning as they set out on their journey. They are on foot, and as they walk they pay careful attention to One who appears to be both leader and teacher. His dress indicates nothing of prestige or ecclesiastical rank, but his words carry weight and penetrate. He is adept at illustrating his messages, finding lessons in nature and daily chores; it has been said that he draws sermons even from stones.

As the sun rises in the sky and the heat becomes somewhat oppressive, conversation wanes, as everyone feels the drudgery of the march and the leader in particular is getting tired. They reach a village at noon and are glad to see that there is a place beside the communal well where they can rest under trees, sitting on large stones. Here the leader lies down on a stone bench, somewhat exhausted by now, and after a few minutes the others leave him while they go to buy a snack at the store. We are surprised that not a single one of them has stayed with the Master, but we soon learn that there is a divine plan behind this solitude.

Not only are the men gone, but other footsteps are heard approaching. They belong to a woman, who is alone and carrying a pitcher on her head. It is strange for her to come at this hour, but she wants to draw water from the well.

If I had the skill of a painter, I would present the picture of an olive grove, old smooth stones at the mouth of the well, the rustic bench and a woman standing in the background, suspicious and obviously wanting to keep her distance from this stranger.

I would put as title: CONTACT; if you want a subtitle, it would be The Searcher and the Wanted.

It is that the one resting by the well was none other than the Lord of Glory who left the courts of heaven to bring divine blessing to sad men and women afflicted by sin, and the one standing there, unbeknownst to her as yet, is one whom He came to seek and to save.

The wise and tender way in which he draws that woman from the paths of sin to the knowledge of him, and the marvelous development of her soul as she advances step by step, until the revelation of God himself enlightens her being, is a story that has thrilled God's people through the centuries.

Parched, He asks her to drink from the cold, refreshing water of the well, but her request only provokes a manifestation of the attitude she has towards Him. It is one of aggressiveness, of open CONTRARY. She shares the childish jealousy and hatred that existed between the Samaritans and the Jews. To her, he is nothing more than a despicable Jew.

His refusal of that request brings out the grace of the man's heart. He says, in effect: "I have asked you for a very simple gift, and you have not answered, but would that you knew what a great gift God wants to give; if you could only realize that He who has humbled Himself to the extreme of asking you for a drink of water is the same Lord of Glory who has come to bring to men the gift of God, then you would have asked Him of Him, and He would have given you living water!"

We are before a beautiful figure of God's salvation: fresh water from a spring in a parched land; divine life, love and freedom emanating in the soul that has known the drought of the world and the annoyance of sin.

His unexpected words surprise the woman. She renounces antagonism and feels a great CURIOSITY, accompanied by a marked sense of respect. She addresses Him as Lord (*kurios*). He must have been a great personage, possibly even greater than our ancestral hero, Jacob. But how can he give water, when he has nothing to draw it with and the well is deep (45 meters, it is said)?

His surprise gives him the opportunity to contrast the blessing God offers with the best the world can give. The pleasures of the world, sinful or not, are ephemeral and soon pass away. They cannot give lasting satisfaction. But the blessing God gives is perennial, of lasting, eternal satisfaction. "Whosoever drinketh of the water that I shall give him shall never thirst."

Her attention is intense; in her heart there is now a CONFLICT. Involuntarily, she assumes the place of supplicant: "Give me," she exclaims. "Give me that living water!" She had drunk amply of worldly pleasures and knew they were lacking when she wanted them most. She had sought happiness and found fallacy. And now a wonderful Stranger has come to meet her; his words have awakened new desires in her heart.

He, the divine Giver, has offered her the greatest of blessings, and she responds with the cry, "Give me that living water!" What more is needed? Why does she not do it at once? Ah, it is that there is an obstacle. Before the human heart can receive God's gift, that obstacle must be removed. It is called sin. All sin must be brought to light and condemned, before God can give His living water.

With the unmistakable skill of a highly trained surgeon, He puts His finger on the sore spot in that woman's life, and with a few penetrating words lays before her conscience the whole black history of her self-gratification and sin.

As he listens, the arrow of CONVICTION reaches his heart. "I perceive," he says, "that you are a prophet." She feels that God has spoken to her through the Stranger by the well, exposing all the sinfulness of her life. What can she do, is there anything she can offer to God to clear the record? Yes, strange as it may seem, this woman has her religion. She has worshipped God on Mount Gerizim, a place of renowned antiquity, the sanctuary of greatest tradition in Palestine. She speaks of this to the Unknown and brings up for debate the controversy with Jews over where one should worship.

Very graciously He responds to their difficulties. No doubt the Jewish system was ordained of God, but all earthly ritual was about to disappear. The emphasis now is not the place of worship but the Person to be worshipped - the Father revealed in His only begotten Son.

These words produce the COLLAPSE of the whole scaffolding in which his soul trusted. His religion was vain. He had trusted in a rotten support and now that he puts it to the test, it does not resist. And are there not many today who make the same mistake? A certain Christian woman offered a priest of Rome an evangelical booklet, and he refused, protesting, "I have my religion." Respectfully she replied: "And I have Christ". Those words entered like a dart into the soul of that gentleman and proved to be the first step in the conviction that led to his confession of Jesus as Savior.

Great was the change that a few minutes' conversation wrought in this woman; disdain and curiosity seemed a thing of the past. There she stands with a great conflict in her soul, a longing for the blessing that has been offered her, her life of sin consuming her conscience and her religion in shreds at her feet. What remedy will there be?

There is only one. She had heard of the promised Messiah; the prophets had spoken of that wonderful Person whom God was going to send. When He comes, He will abolish all evil, explain all mysteries, remove all sorrow, bring peace to the troubled, strength to the weak and forgiveness to the penitent. He is her only resource; only the promised Christ of God can supply what she needs.

And in that moment of despair the heavenly Visitor reveals Himself: "I am He who speaks to you".

The flash of revelation enlightens the poor woman's soul and brings peace, joy and blessing to her heart. This is true CONVERSION. It is the heartfelt reception of the Lord Jesus Christ and the personal, intimate relationship with Him. Filled with her new-found joy, she hurries home to tell her wonderful experience to the neighbors. So well has she caught the Master's Spirit that her first word of testimony is the one that was always on His lips: "Come to me," said the Savior of sinners. She for her part cries out: "Come and see". To see One who told me all that I have done. "Is not this the Christ?" It was; it is.

She then goes on to give a forceful CONFESSION of His Name. Many believed in Him because of her words, and like any true evangelist she would be overjoyed to hear them say: "We no longer believe only because of what you have said, for we ourselves have heard, and we know that this is indeed the Savior of the world, the Christ".

Conclusion

The Gospel of John is a masterpiece of narrative, deeply imbued with the divine spirit. It stirs our emotions and sharpens our senses to convey the truth that Jesus Christ is the Son of God sent to save the world. The apostle John understood the Lord's message well and gently cried out to our hearts so that we too might hear it. He exhorts us to believe and have eternal life, convincing us by his words of the reality of the loving gospel of Jesus. There is no better doctrine than the convincing, faithful and unmistakable testimony of the apostle John.

With these varied characteristics, the Gospel of John reflects the author's deep devotion to his Lord. In doing so, it enriches us with a unique vision that captures the purity of Christ's love, shining even more brightly through the eyes of one who came to know him as intimately as the apostle John. This work provides an outstanding testimony compiled during those early Christian days, making it a precious treasure for Christians and all those in search of a reliable reference for spiritual health.

Don't miss out!

Visit the website below and you can sign up to receive emails whenever Bible Sermons publishes a new book. There's no charge and no obligation.

https://books2read.com/r/B-A-MZBS-EPGGC

BOOKS2READ

Connecting independent readers to independent writers.

Did you love *Analyzing Notes in the Book of John: John's Contribution to the New Testament Scriptures*? Then you should read *Analyzing the Education of Labor in Genesis: The Purpose of Life on Earth*[1] by Bible Sermons!

The Bible makes it clear that work is important to God. This applies to any profession or occupation of one, *from being a father or mother, bus driver, artist, engineer, etc.* Following are key Biblical teachings on work from the book of Genesis to Revelation, offering practical guidance for Christians who wonder where the Bible stands on how we should approach our work. **The book of Genesis is essential to understanding the biblical teaching on work.** It tells the story of God's creation and how He provides humans with the tools necessary to work. In Genesis, we see God at work and learn that His plan for

---

1. https://books2read.com/u/3yW7jp

2. https://books2read.com/u/3yW7jp

us is that we also work. The book teaches us about the importance of obeying and disobeying God in our work, and how God works in both our obedience and our disobedience. It is the foundation of all biblical teaching on work and is essential to understanding the other books of the Bible.

Also by Bible Sermons

Notes in the New Testament

Analyzing Notes in the Book of Matthew: Fulfillments of Old Testament Prophecies

Analyzing Notes in the Book of Mark: Finding Peace in Difficult Times

Analyzing Notes in the Book of Luke: The Divine Love of Jesus Revealed

Analyzing Notes in the Book of John: John's Contribution to the New Testament Scriptures

Overflying The Bible

Bible Introduction: Overflying The Bible from Genesis by Brethren in the Faith

Chronological Prophecy: Things That Will Happen on Earth

Bible Study: Genesis 1. Creation in Six Days

The Education of Labor in the Bible

Analyzing the Teaching of Labor in Exodus: From Slavery to Liberation

About the Author

This bible study series is perfect for Christians of any level, from children to youth to adults. It provides an engaging and interactive way to learn the Bible, with activities and discussion topics that will help deepen your understanding of scripture and strengthen your faith. Whether you're a beginner or an experienced Christian, this series will help you grow in your knowledge of the Bible and strengthen your relationship with God. Led by brothers with exemplary testimonies and extensive knowledge of scripture, who congregate in the name of the Lord Jesus Christ throughout the world.

About the Publisher

Editor

Elvis A. Betancourt T. 4135 Stoney Creek Dr., Lincolnton, NC 28092 *elvisbetancourtt@gmail.com*

Contáctenos

Preguntas y comentarios generales: *seminitt25@gmail.com*